GLORY'S TREASURES

A JOURNEY THROUGH THE ALPHABET

WRITTEN BY Joanne M. Pierre

ILLUSTRATED BY Wei Wei Chan

Glory's Treasures: A Journey Through the Alphabet
© 2021 by Grace Covenant Books LLC

Library of Congress Control Number: 2021916636

ISBN: 978-1-7367440-0-0 (Paperback)
       978-1-7367440-1-7 (Hardcover)
       978-1-7367440-3-1 (E-book)

To learn more about our books, visit us at:
www.GraceCovenantBooks.com

This book is dedicated to

My Rock, Redeemer, and Sustainer.
My Lord and Savior, Jesus Christ,
who is the Lord over my life.

To my wonderful husband,
Patrick, who has been my biggest
cheerleader, I love you dearly.

To my three beautiful children:
Grace, Jeremiah, and Hannah;
I love you all. Remember that with
Christ all things are possible.

Lastly, to my amazing family and
friends, who believed in my vision
and love for children.

Once there was a young girl named Glory. Glory loved to spend time with her family. She especially loved attending church services with her parents and younger brother, Josiah. She loved walking into church, listening to the pianist and choir members sing their tunes. She loved seeing all her friends and the friendly faces greeting her at the start of the service.

Most of all, Glory loved listening to her Sunday school teacher, Ms. Charis, reading Bible stories. Ms. Charis had a way of making Bible stories come to life. As Ms. Charis read Bible stories, Glory could imagine herself in every scene.

One Sunday, during the church service, Ms. Charis exclaimed in a cheerful voice, "Today we are going to memorize scriptures from the Bible!" Then Ms. Charis pulled out a wooden box that contained brightly-colored flash cards. Each card had one letter of the alphabet. As Ms. Charis read each letter, she connected it with a Bible verse. When Ms. Charis began reading the cards, Glory no longer saw herself in the classroom. Suddenly, Glory was immersed in the scenes of the scriptures.

He will order His *Angels*
to protect you wherever you go

Psalm 91:11 NLT

Glory watched with amazement as she saw majestic angels surrounding her. The angels were dressed in the most magnificent white. They stood tall, with authority. The angels held bright swords. Glory felt protected.

Give unto the LORD the glory due unto His name. Worship the LORD in the Beauty of holiness.

Psalm 29:2 KJV

Glory was suddenly pulled into a lovely scene of the beauty of creation. She could see colorful birds and animals that smiled at her arrival. Then Glory noticed some animals gazing at a bright light and worshiping. "The light is bright and pure!" Glory thought.

Jesus stood up and said to the storm,
"Peace, be still!" The wind ceased,
and there was a great Calm.

Mark 4:39 ESV

As Ms. Charis read the next Bible verse, Glory felt a drop of water
on her face. She found herself in the middle of the sea, in a large boat.
The boat shook violently from the big waves and strong winds. Glory
saw men on the boat who looked afraid. They hurried to wake up Jesus,
who was sleeping in the back of the boat. Glory watched as Jesus
got up peacefully and spoke to the sea. The sea was suddenly calm.

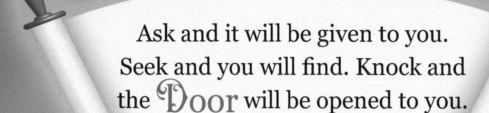

Ask and it will be given to you.
Seek and you will find. Knock and
the Door will be opened to you.

Matthew 7:7 NIV

Glory raised her hand and asked, "Ms. Charis, where can I find the door that the verse is talking about?"

"Well, Glory," Ms. Charis answered. "This is a heavenly door that we cannot see. Christ is using a story to tell us that you can call on Him and ask whatever you need, and He will answer you."

Oh LORD, our lord, how **Excellent** is Your name in all the earth.

Psalm 8:9 NKJV

Ms. Charis continued reading with a smile. She pulled out another brightly-colored card from the wooden box. As she read, Glory immediately saw the vibrant colors of a rainbow. She was surrounded by the beautiful colors and the rainbow lifted her high up into the sky. Looking down, she could see all the people, clouds, and scenery.

Ms. Charis continued to read the next few cards. As she read, she reminded the class how important they all are in the eyes of God. She also reminded them that they were carefully made by God and they can do all things through Christ. Glory felt confident after hearing Ms. Charis read those verses. She felt like a champion!

I praise you because I am ℱearfully and wonderfully made. Your works are wonderful. I know that full well.

Psalm 139:14 NIV

For I can do everything through Christ who 𝒢ives me strength.

Philippians 4:13 NLT

Ms. Charis suddenly cried out, "H is for Hosanna!" Startled, Glory looked up and smiled at Ms. Charis. As Ms. Charis read the next few verses, Glory imagined herself in a Holy City. She intently watched as Jesus rode into the city, riding on a donkey. People lined the streets to worship Him. Glory could hear their shouts of, "Hosanna!"

Hosanna!
Blessed is He who
comes in the name
of the LORD!

Mark 11:9 ESV

Imitate God in
everything you do,
because you are His
dear children.

Ephesians 5:1 NLT

The works of His hands
are truth and Justice.
All His instructions are
trustworthy.

Psalm 111:7 CSB

The LORD bless you
and Keep you.

Numbers 6:24 ESV

Each time Ms. Charis read the verses they
came alive. Glory could feel herself in the
scenes. She felt a sudden warmth and
protection as she heard Bible verses J and K.
She felt loved. It felt like the hands of God
were embracing her.

For God so **Loved** the world, that He gave His only Son, that whoever believes in Him should not perish but have eternal life.

John 3:16 ESV

Praise Him, sun and **Moon**! Praise Him, all you stars of light!

Psalm 148:3 NKJV

Ms. Charis continued with Bible verses L and M. Glory saw herself lifted up into space. "Wow!" Glory thought as she looked at the brightness of the stars, moon, and planets. Glory looked with amazement and could see the Earth far away. She noticed a big heart surrounding it.

When Glory heard Bible verses N and O, she remembered all the scrumptious dinners she had with her family. They did not always have much, but Glory ate with joy and contentment because every day they had food to eat.

Your Father knows exactly
what you **Need**, even
before you ask Him.

Matthew 6:8 NLT

Our Father in heaven,
may Your name be
honored as holy.

Matthew 6:9 CSB

As Ms. Charis read Bible verses P and Q, Glory could hear the sounds of praising, singing, and worship coming from the sanctuary. She could hear the choir singing "Holy, Holy, LORD God Almighty." She could hear all the different voices and the beautiful melodies of many instruments.

Let everything that has breath praise the LORD. **P**raise the LORD!

Psalm 150:6 NKJV

He will **Q**uiet you with His love, He will rejoice over you with singing.

Zephaniah 3:17 NKJV

He is not here. He is **Risen**, as He said He would. Come and see the place where the LORD lay.

Matthew 28:6 NKJV

Whoever calls on the name of the LORD shall be **Saved**."

Romans 10:13 NKJV

Glory could not wait for Ms. Charis to read the next few cards. As Ms. Charis pulled out the cards and started reading, Glory heard what sounded like an earthquake. She could see the empty tomb with what looked like a bright light at the entrance.

Trust in the LORD with all your heart. Do not lean on your own understanding.

Proverbs 3:5 ESV

He will cover you with His feathers, and Under His wings you will find refuge.

Psalm 91:4 NIV

Card by card and verse by verse, Ms. Charis continued to read.
Each time, Glory was full of joy and faith.

Very truly I tell you, the one who believes has eternal life.

John 6:47 NIV

Whoever believes in me, as the scripture has said, out of his heart will flow rivers of living Water.

John 7:38 ESV

Glory truly enjoyed hearing the Bible verses and liked imagining all the different places the scriptures could take her.

...LET US EXALT HIS NAME TOGETHER.

YOUR WORD IS A LAMP...

Magnify the LORD with me. Let us eXalt His name together.

Psalm 34:3 ESV

Your word is a lamp to my feet. It is a light on my path.

Psalm 119:105 NIV

As Ms. Charis read the verses for X and Y, Glory suddenly saw herself in a forest. Walking along the dark path she felt frightened. "It's so dark," she thought. But as she heard the words Ms. Charis read, the path lit up. The light seemed to come from all the letters of the scriptures Ms. Charis had read to her earlier. She began to bravely walk through the darkness, staying on the well-lit path, as the scriptures went before her.

PSALM 34:3 ESV

... LIGHT ON MY PATH

PSALM 119:105 NIV

"Alright boys and girls, this final verse is very important," said Ms. Charis. Glory could hardly wait for Bible verse Z. Ms. Charis continued, "This verse reminds us to always be eager when serving the Lord."
Our final verse for today is...

Never be lacking in Zeal,
but keep your spiritual fervor,
serving the Lord

Romans 12:11 NIV

Just then Glory's parents came to pick her and Josiah up from the children's church. Glory could not wait for the next children's service. She wondered what Ms. Charis would talk about next week.

ABOUT THE AUTHOR

JOANNE M. PIERRE is a daughter, wife, mom, author, and creative who has dedicated her life to service. She earned a bachelor's degree in nursing and a master's degree in nursing education. Joanne is a registered nurse and serves at a non-profit organization in New York City, helping the most vulnerable communities. Outside of Joanne's vocational career, her passions lie in serving children and youth.

Joanne wants to inspire children to feel loved, special, and confident about who they are. Joanne hopes that her books will encourage children to see the world through the lens of Christ's love. Joanne serves with her supportive husband who is a youth pastor at their local church. Together they have three incredible children. Joanne hopes to encourage children and youth to live out Christ's mandate from Matthew 5:16, to let their light shine before men and bring glory to their Heavenly Father.

CPSIA information can be obtained
at www.ICGtesting.com
Printed in the USA
BVHW021915171021
619166BV00007B/108